CELEBRATING ALL CULTURES

BY ABBY COLICH

BLUE OWL
BOOKS

TIPS FOR CAREGIVERS

Social and emotional learning (SEL) helps children manage emotions, learn how to feel empathy, create and achieve goals, and make good decisions. Strong lessons and support in SEL will help children establish positive habits in communication, cooperation, and decision-making. By incorporating SEL in early reading, children will learn the importance of accepting and celebrating all people in their communities.

BEFORE READING

Talk to the reader about culture. Explain that culture has to do with our ways of life. Give examples of different aspects of culture.

Discuss: Can you name some parts of your culture? How would you describe your culture? Can you name a part of someone else's culture?

AFTER READING

Talk to the reader about ways he or she can celebrate cultural differences with others.

Discuss: What is one way you can accept another person's culture? Why should we accept others? Why is it good for a community to celebrate all people?

SEL GOAL

Children may have a loose understanding of acceptance. Talk to readers about the importance of empathy in accepting and celebrating the differences of others, especially as they pertain to one's culture. Ask them to think about a time when they felt left out and a time when they felt included. Then ask readers to consider the feelings they had in both situations. Make a list of the feelings they had when they were accepted and included and the feelings they had when they were singled out for being different. Explain that our communities are better when everyone is accepted and included.

TABLE OF CONTENTS

CHAPTER 1

WHAT IS CULTURE?

Have you seen foods from a different part of the world at the grocery store? Maybe you've tried foods from different countries.

kebab

taco

pho

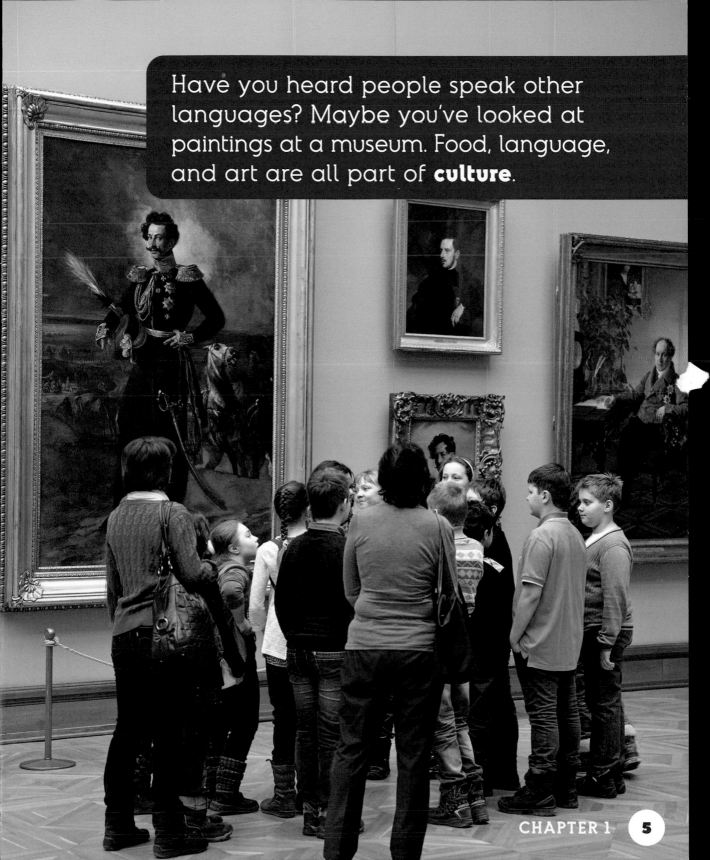

Have you heard people speak other languages? Maybe you've looked at paintings at a museum. Food, language, and art are all part of **culture**.

Culture is a way of life. It is what makes us who we are. Music, clothing, and celebrations are all part of culture. So is how people act and **behave**. Do you hug people when you greet them? This is part of your culture!

LEARN YOUR CULTURE

We learn our culture from others. We can learn it from our family or others in our **community**. Do you learn how to make certain foods? That is part of your culture, too!

Diwali celebration

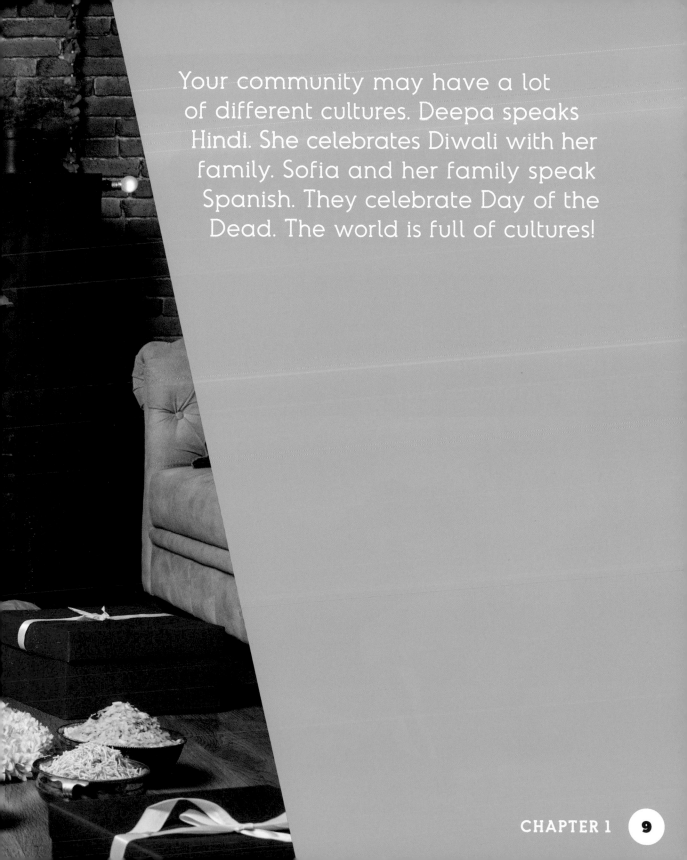

Your community may have a lot of different cultures. Deepa speaks Hindi. She celebrates Diwali with her family. Sofia and her family speak Spanish. They celebrate Day of the Dead. The world is full of cultures!

When we learn more about or **experience** other cultures, it helps us respect them. Kim listens to music from another part of the world. She looks up videos to see how people dance to it!

READ ABOUT IT!

Another way to learn about other cultures is to read about them. Not sure where to look? Ask a teacher or librarian! You can share what you learn with your family, friends, and classmates.

Do you know someone who celebrates another culture? Ask him or her about it. Find the similarities and differences between your cultures. You may find out that you are more alike than you think. Getting to know others can help you **appreciate** other cultures and your own.

WHAT TO SAY

Show respect and **empathy** when asking about someone's culture. Don't respond by saying theirs is different or weird. Just because it's different from yours doesn't mean it deserves less respect. One culture is not better than another. You could say, "Oh, that's interesting! Can you tell me more?"

CHAPTER 3

SHARE AND CELEBRATE

You can share your culture with others in many ways. Charlie's school is having culture night. Charlie shows others how to do a hip-hop dance.

Maya teaches her classmates sign language. Some are nervous they will mess up. Maya **encourages** them to try it with her. She has **patience** with them and slows down the signs.

Shan is Chinese. Her friends come to her birthday party. She eats very long noodles to celebrate. Emma is Australian. At her birthday party, she shows her friends how to make fairy bread. How do you celebrate birthdays?

fairy
bread

Culture is everywhere. It is part of our everyday lives. Learning about other cultures is fun! And it helps us understand and appreciate others and ourselves.

Whether at school, on a sports team, or at work when you grow up, you'll have to work with all sorts of people. Get to know them! When we accept everyone, we can work together to accomplish so much.

GOALS AND TOOLS

GROW WITH GOALS

Accepting all people, no matter their culture, is important. You can help others learn more about your culture, too!

Goal: Can you name some things that are part of your culture? What are some things about your culture that you would like to share with someone else?

Goal: What do you want to know about another culture? How can you learn this?

Goal: Get to know someone you haven't spoken with much before. Try to find things you have in common or that you both like.

WRITING REFLECTION

Knowing about your own culture can help you accept other cultures.

1. What is your favorite part about your culture?

2. What is something from another culture you want to learn more about?

3. What can you do to be more accepting of others?

GLOSSARY

appreciate
To enjoy or value somebody or something.

behave
To act in a particular way.

community
A group of people who all have something in common.

culture
The ideas, customs, traditions, and way of life of a group of people.

empathy
The ability to understand and be sensitive to the thoughts and feelings of others.

encourages
Gives someone confidence, usually by using praise and support.

experience
To participate in events in order to gain knowledge.

patience
The ability to put up with problems or delays without getting angry or upset.

TO LEARN MORE

Finding more information is as easy as 1, 2, 3.

1. Go to www.factsurfer.com
2. Enter "**celebratingallcultures**" into the search box.
3. Choose your cover to see a list of websites.

INDEX

Blue Owl Books are published by Jump!, 5357 Penn Avenue South, Minneapolis, MN 55419, www.jumplibrary.com

Library of Congress Cataloging-in-Publication Data

Names: Colich, Abby, author.
Title: Celebrating all cultures / Abby Colich.
Description: Minneapolis: Jump!, Inc., 2021.
Series: Celebrating our communities | Includes index.
Audience: Ages 7–10. | Audience: Grades 2–3.
Identifiers: LCCN 2019059128 (print)
LCCN 2019059129 (ebook)
ISBN 9781645273653 (hardcover)
ISBN 9781645273660 (paperback)
ISBN 9781645273677 (ebook)
Subjects: LCSH: Social learning–Juvenile literature. | Affective education–Juvenile literature.
Communities–Social aspects–Juvenile literature. | Cultural pluralism–Juvenile literature.
Classification: LCC HQ783 .C65 2021 (print) | LCC HQ783 (ebook) | DDC 303.3/2–dc23
LC record available at https://lccn.loc.gov/2019059128
LC ebook record available at https://lccn.loc.gov/2019059129

Editor: Jenna Gleisner
Designer: Michelle Sonnek

Photo Credits: Photodsindia.com/SuperStock, cover (left); DiversityStudio/Shutterstock, cover (right); Mega Pixel/Shutterstock, 1 (top left); Bayanova Svetlana/Shutterstock, 1 (bottom left); Maxim Chipenko/Shutterstock, 1 (right); sirikorn thamniyom/Shutterstock, 3; GSDesign/Shutterstock, 4 (left); bonchan/Shutterstock, 4 (middle); DNY59/iStock, 4 (right); Popova Valeriya/Shutterstock, 5; klebercordeiro/iStock, 6–7; StockImageFactory.com/Shutterstock, 8–9; Thinkstock/Getty, 10; FatCamera/iStock, 11; SeventyFour/Shutterstock, 12–13; LightField Studios/Shutterstock, 14–15; Alfa Photostudio/Shutterstock, 16; Hugh Sitton/Getty, 17; Brent Hofacker/Shutterstock, 18–19; kali9/iStock, 20–21.

Printed in the United States of America at Corporate Graphics in North Mankato, Minnesota.